How to Stop Being a Perfectionist

A 30-Day Plan to Control Negative Thoughts,
Eliminate Analysis Paralysis,

and Increase Productivity.

Steven Schuster

steveschusterbooks@gmail.com

www.stevenschusterbooks.com

Copyright © 2021 by Steven Schuster. All rights reserved.

No part of this publication may be reproduced, stored in a retrieval system, or transmitted in any form or by any means, electronic, mechanical, photocopying, recording, scanning or otherwise, except as permitted under Section 107 or 108 of the 1976 United States Copyright Act, without the prior written permission of the author.

Limit of Liability/ Disclaimer of Warranty: The author makes no representations or warranties with respect to the accuracy or completeness of the contents of this work and specifically disclaims all warranties, including without limitation warranties of fitness for a particular purpose. No warranty may be created or extended by sales or promotional materials.

The advice and recipes contained herein may not be suitable for everyone. This work is sold with the understanding that the author is not engaged in rendering medical, legal or other professional advice or services. If professional assistance is required, the services of a competent professional person should be sought. The author shall not be liable for damages arising herefrom. The fact that an individual, organization of website is referred to in this work as a citation and/or potential source of further information does not mean that the author endorses the information the individual, organization to website may provide or recommendations they/it may make. Further, readers should be aware that Internet websites listed in this work might have changed or disappeared between when this work was written and when it is read.

For general information on the products and services or to obtain technical support, please contact the author.

FREE BOOK ALERT

Visit www.stevenschusterbooks.com to download your FREE EBOOK, The Misguided Mind! Get fascinated by the depth of our own cognitive biases!

TABLE OF CONTENTS

Introduction 11

Chapter 1: How Does The Perfectionist Mind Work? 17

Chapter 2: Why Is Perfectionism Bad For You? What Are The Good Parts? 37

Chapter 3: Negative Side Effects Of Perfectionism 55

Chapter 4: How To Overcome Perfectionist Habits 69

Chapter 5: How To Heal The Perfectionist Soul 107

Chapter 6: How Much Of A Perfectionist Are You? 153

Chapter 7: The 30-Day Perfectionism Cure 167

Closing 207

Reference 209

Endnotes 211

Introduction

Are you harder on yourself than everyone else? Do you hold yourself to incredibly high standards and are disappointed with yourself when you fail to meet them? Do you find that sometimes those self-imposed standards put so much pressure on you that they can actually end up holding you back? If so, then your perfectionism might be working overtime. While this may seem like an average problem, it can become a pervasive presence that will slowly sabotage your growth and limit your potential.

Perfectionism has a twin brother, you see, called procrastination. In most cases, they show up together. They are like misbehaving children, enforcing each other in their deeds. Perfectionism may say, "This is not done well enough. I can't give this work out from my hands." Procrastination would reply, "Damn right, let's just sit around and think about how we could improve this work. But in the meantime, let's have a snack, it helps with thinking. Also, let's take a nap, our brain needs rest. How about some entertainment? No wonder our thinking is so dry. We haven't had a good laugh in ages." And on and on it goes.

Procrastination is the ultimate road to hell paved with good intentions. No one ever procrastinates without a good reason—or should I rather say, a well-rounded rationalization. Our thinking mind is tricky that way; it can provide a convincing explanation as to why we should or shouldn't do something. How does the thinking mind decide which action it will defend? Well, our emotional mind is the judge of that.

NYU psychologist and the author of the book *The Happiness Hypothesis*, Jonathan Haidt explained this phenomenon with the metaphor of the rider and the elephant. Our emotional mind is the elephant, the thinking mind is the rider. While the rider of the elephant seems to be in charge, when there's a disagreement between them, the elephant usually prevails.

Chip and Dan Heath expand on this metaphor in their book, *Switch: How to Change Things When Change Is Hard*. They argue that the rider (the thinking mind) is responsible for planning and direction. But it often falls into the trap of overthinking, trying to motivate the elephant (the emotional mind) to get things done and avoid instant gratification. It's an exhausting business. In psychology, we call this phenomenon willpower depletion. We consume all of our rational, delayed gratification-bound credits over time. This is why it is more likely that we will likely choose cookies instead of baby carrots to snack on in the evening.

Procrastination is the favorite pastime of the elephant. And a comfortable go-to place. We learn to procrastinate as early as childhood. We leave our homework to the last minute because we watch TV. We get out of bed just before the school bus arrives because we stayed up late finishing our homework. We even observe our parents putting off tasks, so we have a lot of fertile ground to adopt this bad habit from and practice it. Procrastination rolls over into our adulthood. We postpone important tasks and choose immediate gratification instead. It feels better in the moment, doesn't it?

We invent all sorts of creative reasons why we procrastinate. Still, it can really be broken down to just a handful of emotionally motivated reasons in reality. We fear failure. We fear judgment. We fear to prove to others (and ourselves) that we don't measure up. We fear imperfection. We feel too much pressure to perform, so we avert our focus from the task at hand counterintuitively. Some are just simply bad at time management. If you recognized yourself in these, worry not. This book will strive to distill the ways the perfectionist mind works. You will discover the positives and negatives that can come from being a perfectionist and what you can do about it.

This journey will leave you with a greater understanding of yourself. You will be able to overcome the challenges of perfectionism with a simple yet powerful 30-day program. Get ever closer to reaching your full potential and living the productive, prosperous life you deserve.

Chapter 1: How Does the Perfectionist Mind Work?

Dory, a computer model designer, considered herself a person with a growth mindset. She was never satisfied with the work she produced. Day after day, she scrutinized her projects, finding flaws in the color choices, template layout, size and font of the letters, and so on. She was the first to arrive and last to leave her office. Despite her outstanding hard work, she never got a promotion, and her boss instead scolded her when she turned in her projects late. The boss didn't care so much about the immaculate symmetry, the Rembrandt-shaming color composition, and extremely well-matched font-letter sizing. He just wanted good enough, but punctual, work.

Despite telling Dory repeatedly, she didn't seem to get why her boss was critical of her. She felt inadequate, and in her mind, the problem was that she didn't do a perfect enough job. So, each time, she put some more work into the project and delivered it even later. Dory was struggling with a vicious reinforcing loop of perfectionism. She was blindsided with the fact that her striving for providing perfect work was the problem. She hated her job, her boss, and ultimately herself for being so deficient.

Why do we want to be perfect? Some people think Martha Stewart's ideas on entertaining and decorating or the influence of online platforms like Pinterest or Instagram are to blame. In reality, all these sites highlight the perfection gap people have always worried about by making it more visible in popular culture.

We compare ourselves to others. We want to live up to the images we create in our own mind about the work we want to deliver, the lives we wish and expect for ourselves. The problem is that these images are often unrealistic, impractical, and have such high standards that they are impossible to meet. They can make us very hard on ourselves when we fail to reach them. And we do fail.

So what is the driving force behind Dory's insatiable desire to achieve perfection? It can vary from person to person, but it is often rooted in fear of failure or a deep-seated feeling of not being good enough.

Those who fear failure often see themselves and their lives through a very rigid lens. Things are cut and dried from their viewpoint. They have either succeeded, or they have failed. There is no middle ground when it comes to the way they judge themselves. People with perfectionist tendencies are so afraid to fail that they keep working harder and harder to achieve perfection. Since their goal doesn't really exist, success keeps escaping them just beyond their grasp.

Another common reason people are driven to achieve the unachievable is that they see themselves as not good enough. This feeling of inadequacy does not have to have any empirical basis. They believe it, so in their mind, it is definitively true. Perfectionist people worry excessively about how others view them and are afraid to make mistakes because they assume it will make others think less of them. Thus, they try to avoid making mistakes at all costs. If they could only attain perfection, they would prove to themselves and everyone else that they're worthy. Perfectionism is an impossibly high standard to live up to, and pursuing it can prove exhausting.

Another reason some people may be perfectionists is out of a desire to gain control. There is a lot of chaos in the world, and so much of it is beyond their control. In a desire to find something they can control, they may take things to the extreme. They want the perfect car, home, or office. They think it should be pristine, and they will work at it continuously to keep the outward appearance perfect. Things never remain pristine for long.

They have to continually try to keep up with an unrealistic and unsustainable expectation of perfection.

Types of Perfectionism

There are many different types of perfectionism. They all fall into one of two categories: adaptive or maladaptive. There is some debate amongst those who study perfectionism as to whether it is possible to call any type adaptive. Still, for the purpose of our discussion here, we will attempt to distinguish between the two.

Adaptive perfectionism has people striving to reach very high standards, but with one major distinction—they understand that expecting to achieve perfection is an impossibly high standard that no one can actually get. People who are adaptive perfectionists are pleased with themselves when they put great effort into achieving their goals.

Adaptive perfectionism might lead someone to put a lot of time and effort into planning a big party. They might work very hard to make the party as exquisite as they possibly can. Still, they would understand that the party's chances of going off without a hitch and everything being absolutely perfect are very slim. They would be satisfied with how much time and effort they put into the party's planning and preparation. Adaptive perfectionists seem to respond better when things go wrong and tend to feel less stressed out and upset than maladaptive perfectionists.

In the example above, the party planner was actually striving for excellence—not perfection.

There is no harm in wanting to take pride in a job well done or holding yourself to high standards and having great expectations for what you feel you should accomplish. In fact, that can make you motivated and driven to achieve your goals. Where people run into problems is when the line between wanting and expecting excellence and perfection becomes blurred. We see this often in high-performing athletes. They may begin striving for excellence. But as they experience success in their sport, they may increase their pressure to maintain their success by never making a misstep. Counterintuitively, this approach puts so much stress on them that they will, in fact, do something wrong and sabotage their success. Then their future depends on whether or not they realize that perfectionism brought trouble upon them, not that they didn't try hard enough.

Maladaptive perfectionism is when people hold themselves to impossibly unrealistic standards and expect to always achieve perfection. They are extremely critical and hard on themselves when they don't meet the standards they set. In Dory's case, after each project she delivered late and her boss scolded her, she became increasingly stressed out and suffered from decreased self-esteem and depression. Maladaptive perfectionists see themselves as being in control of everything. When things go wrong, they feel as if the blame lies squarely on their shoulders.

Perfectionists desire to present themselves as flawless and avoid any situation in which they think they will not look good. That is an awful lot of pressure to live up to.

Signs That You Might Be a Perfectionist

While perfectionism can manifest in many ways, there are some common characteristics. How many of these traits do you recognize in yourself?

1. Letting others help you is not your strong suit.

2. You live by the philosophy that if you want something done right, you'd better do it yourself. Delegating tasks to others is not something that comes easily to you because it means you are relinquishing control.

3. Your sense of self and confidence comes from your achievements and the reaction you receive from others.

4. You are always trying to reach high standards of excellence, and you love to get praise from others for a job well done.

5. Once you have accomplished your goal, you are ready to move on to a new one so you can enjoy those feelings again.

6. You find yourself putting off things that you don't feel like you can be successful at, or avoiding them altogether to avoid feeling like a failure.

7. You hold others to the same high standards that you have for yourself. You always give

your best effort, and you are annoyed when others do not do the same.

8. You often view setbacks as a reason to give up altogether. If you are painting a picture and you "mess up," you might decide to completely start over because the painting has already been "ruined."

9. It is hard for you to complete something because you are always looking at it with a critical eye, thinking that there is more you can do to make it better. You don't want anyone to see your work until it's as good as it can possibly be.

10. You view things as being black or white without a lot of room for gray. In your mind, things are either right or wrong—perfect or awful—and there isn't anything in between. If

someone cuts you off in traffic, you view them as rude and inconsiderate rather than someone who made a poor choice or who might have been in a hurry or who had something else on their mind.

11. You have a set of rules in your mind that you think you and everyone else should abide by. You are not happy with yourself or anyone else when they don't behave in a way you think they should.

12. No matter how many things go right, you will always be fixated on the one thing that went wrong. You may have answered forty-nine questions correctly on an exam, but if you made a mistake on one question, that would be the one that receives all of your attention.

13. Many people find joy in the journey. You are not one of them. You are all about achieving results. You put everything you have into reaching your goal. The outcome is your only concern.

14. You are very hard on yourself. You blame yourself when something goes wrong and you have a tough time letting your mistakes go even well after they have happened. You are not quick to forgive yourself and move on.

15. You can find mistakes even when others can't. You are the first to notice them, and you immediately try to fix them. Sometimes the mistakes are really there, and sometimes they exist only in your mind's eye.

My Personal Story with Perfectionism

Why am I writing this book? What gives me any authority to speak on the subject? I have been there and done that. I have walked in those perfectionist shoes. If I am frank, I see many of the characteristics above in myself even today. Am I cured of my perfectionist tendencies? No, and I never will be. However, I am more self-aware and know the thoughts and behaviors that I need to keep my eye out for. When I see them coming to the surface, I act quickly to keep them in check. I am relieved to say that my perfectionism never rose to the level where I felt depressed or suicidal, or kept me from having healthy relationships with others in my life. Still, I can recognize how being a perfectionist has affected my life to the point where I felt unnecessary stress and anxiety. I find it somewhat ironic that it actually ended up holding me back at times and kept me from reaching my full potential in my quest for excellence.

I spent my whole life wanting to do well. I wanted to earn good grades and make myself, my parents, and my teachers proud. I went through school earning all A's and won academic awards, earned scholarships, and delivered the graduation speech in college as valedictorian of my class. It was important to me, and I was willing to work for it. I enjoyed the compliments and praise I received for my hard work and academic abilities. There were many times that I felt stress to maintain the high standards I put on myself. I felt anxiety, thinking my performance might not be good enough. I recognized that I couldn't be perfect. Still, I was hard on myself whenever I wasn't reaching my expectations. I took it to heart and beat myself up over it, vowing to do better the next time, not letting those disappointments go and moving on. During that period in my life, my self-confidence and worth were definitely tied to my academic performance.

Later in life, ironically, my teaching career started my road to becoming a recovering perfectionist. I always strove for excellence in my classroom and was never willing to give less than my best because I wanted to be the best possible teacher. My students deserved that. I began to be seen as a rising star in my school district. I received outstanding evaluations from my students, their parents, my colleagues, and my administrators. I was asked to take on more and more responsibilities and act in a mentoring capacity. I loved helping kids, and I enjoyed receiving accolades for my work. If I ever received a word of criticism from a parent or administrator, I really took it hard and beat myself up over it. It was hard for me to let any negative comments go. Once again, teaching was important to me and my passion, and I was willing to pour my heart and soul into it.

As high-stakes testing began to become more and more of the focus for schools, I saw how stressful it was for my students and colleagues. As a perfectionist, it could easily have been a source of great anxiety for me as well, and on occasion, it was. But I wanted my students and colleagues to make life easier, not stress so much, and be generally happier. How could I expect them to relax and not put so much pressure on themselves if I couldn't do the same? This was also around the same time that my wife and I were starting our family. I knew I wanted to ease up on myself and raise my kids, knowing that it was okay to make mistakes and be human rather than perfect. That meant I had to set the example through my actions. It was time to become more mindful about the behavior I wanted others to model.

Was it easy? No, I had to commit to it and put in the effort daily to keep those perfectionist characteristics in check. Did I have setbacks? Absolutely, but instead of making me want to give up, they make me want to try again to overcome them. The first rule of thumb: don't try to be perfect at ditching perfectionism.

Key Takeaways:

• Perfectionism manifests differently, but these are all defined by having high, often unrealistic standards and expectations. When those standards are not reached, it can lead to undue stress, anxiety, reduced self-esteem and confidence, unhealthy relationships, eating disorders, or even depression.

• Most perfectionists share many of the same characteristics, such as being overly fixated on perceived mistakes or criticism, procrastination and avoidance of things they think they will be unsuccessful at, and getting their self-esteem from their achievements and the way others react to them.

• Overcoming perfectionism is a lifelong process. Becoming more self-aware and quicker to react when you notice your perfectionist tendencies getting out of hand are essential steps toward becoming a recovering perfectionist.

Chapter 2: Why Is Perfectionism Bad for You? What Are the Good Parts?

You might ask yourself, "What is wrong with setting high standards and wanting to achieve excellence?" Nothing, no one should have the goal of performing poorly on a task. As long as there aren't negative consequences that occur as a result, it is healthy to strive for doing your best. But if you place overly high and often unrealistic standards on yourself that you are unable to reach, and become self-loathing or even depressed by it, that's unhealthy. Perfectionists are overly critical of themselves and often compare themselves to others, convinced that they simply don't measure up.

People who hold themselves to impossibly high expectations may suffer at work by taking too long to complete tasks, either because they put off beginning them in a timely manner or because they hold on to projects until they are satisfied that they are the best they can be, like Dory. Spending more time completing work might mean they have less time to enjoy with family and friends. Perfectionism can lead to anxiety and depression and a diminished quality of life.

Accepting your humanity and the fact that you are not now, and can never hope to be, perfect is the first step toward overcoming perfectionism and all of the negative things that go with it. When you recognize the irony that striving for perfection actually holds you back from achieving your full potential and living your best life, you are making progress toward breaking free of your perfectionist characteristics.

Need for Approval, People Pleasing

Perfectionists are stuck on a treadmill that they can't escape. They keep repeating the same pattern over and over. They set impossibly high standards for themselves, inevitably making mistakes because they are human, and then beat themselves up for the mistakes they have made. Wash, rinse, and repeat. As they beat themselves up, they express their disappointment at not achieving perfection by comparing themselves to others. They imagine how everyone else would have done better than they did. This all too constant negative voice playing in their heads starts to erode their self-esteem and self-confidence over time. Before they even realize what has happened, they have an attitude of being afraid to take risks or try new things because they are convinced they will be a failure.

We would never find it acceptable for someone to constantly be overly critical and cruel when speaking to others, and yet that is what perfectionists do to themselves all the time. It can make them question their worth, keep them from enjoying the successes they achieve in life, stand in the way of forming and maintaining healthy relationships, cause their performance at work to suffer, and prevent them from growing personally as well as professionally. Words are powerful things, and the critical negative self-talk that perfectionists subject themselves to can have devastating effects.

Perfectionists tend to people-please. They want to accomplish reaching their incredibly high standards, and on top of that, they want to please others in the process. They want to feel like others approve of and value them. These thus far are not crazy wishes. Most people do want to feel loved, appreciated, and admired by their peers. But people who suffer from perfectionism outright hate the feeling of disappointing anyone. The approval of those who recognize their achievements is the bar against which they measure their own value and self-worth. Their sense of self is closely tied to the way they think others perceive them. Craving praise and acceptance will push them to go to great lengths to attain it. Praise and reassurance makes them feel worthy and like they measure up to others, erasing their insecurities at least for a little while. In order to receive the praise that confirms they are "good enough," perfectionists are willing to constantly put the needs of others above their own. Their inability to say no to others often results in them being taken for granted or taken advantage of. In extreme cases, requiring the constant validation from others can make some people lose sight of who they are and what is really important to them in life.

Concern over Mistakes and Risks

The only way we can grow is if we push ourselves beyond what is comfortable to us. It is then that we can challenge ourselves and reach new heights. For perfectionists, this is a scary thought. They thrive in the known and crave the certainty because they feel in control and think they can be successful. Once they move beyond their comfort zones, they are in uncharted territory and the fear of taking a risk becomes consuming. They think they are likely to fail. That is absolutely the last thing they want to do.

Risks are everywhere in life. In fact, it is often said without risk there is no reward. Imagine all of the things you would miss out on if you never took a risk. You wouldn't make new friends, try new foods, travel to new places, accept a new job, or begin a new relationship. Perfectionists often miss out on experiencing their lives to the fullest because they are terrified of making a mistake and failing.

My brother has a set of twins who are not identical in looks or personality. They are only three years old, but they can help to make this aversion to risks very evident. I recently went with them to a playground. One of the girls is quite adventurous and showed little fear in trying new things. She was eager to go high on the swing and slide down the highest or curviest slide without a moment's hesitation. She walked up to any kid on the playground and started talking to them, and before you knew it, they were running and playing together. Her sister, on the other hand, is more cautious. She is a thinker, and you can practically see the wheels turning in her head as she considers the risk versus reward. She, too, likes to have fun, and saw her sister enjoying all of the playground equipment, but more often than not, decided that she would rather stick with the things she was comfortable with and knew what she could expect to happen. Despite repeated offers, she opted not to let me push her on the swing and she made her way to the top of a slide only to turn around and walk back down the ladder. When she really pushed herself she let me hold her hands as she went down the slide or had me catch her near the bottom. Her behavior on the playground reminds me of how perfectionists live their lives. They are afraid of new and unknown things, and would rather avoid them altogether than take a risk. Just like my little family member, they just might be missing out on some pretty amazing experiences life has to offer.

Doubts about Taking Action and Making Decisions

The inability to make decisions is a common trait among perfectionists. If they are faced with the possibility of making the wrong choice or no choice at all, they would rather make no choice 99.9% of the time. They are so afraid of making a mistake that they would rather not take any action at all. What they don't realize is that inaction is a choice of its own as well. Being indecisive leaves you stuck right where you are: unable to move forward and grow.

How can you ever hope to learn from your mistakes if you are never willing to make any?

You will recall that perfectionists tend to view the world in black and white with little room for shades of gray or middle ground. They see things as being perfect or terrible, right or wrong, successful or a failure. Things that are unknown are very stressful. It doesn't even have to be a big decision. It might be what shoes they should wear with their outfit, what they order from the menu, or what kind of haircut they should get. Perfectionists definitely sweat the small stuff, and this can lead them to feel great anxiety.

They usually assume the worst-case scenario will happen, but it very rarely does. Most people will not notice the shoes they chose to wear, they will have the opportunity to order many more meals from the menu in the future, and their hair will grow out again in a few weeks if it isn't their favorite haircut. Their decisions are not going to be the end of the world, but being so stuck in a rut certainly has negative consequences.

All-or-Nothing Mentality

The belief of perfectionists that they are better off not doing something if they aren't going to be able to do it perfectly can serve as a great hindrance in their lives. They may have wonderful goals and aspirations that they will never take action on because they are afraid to make mistakes. People who do not have the perfectionist mindset are willing to make mistakes because they realize that mistakes are inevitable and a necessary part of their growth and progress. Perfectionists do not see mistakes as obstacles that can be worked through and overcome. Instead, they see the potential for making mistakes to be a reason to avoid starting projects or to quit them before they are complete. This mindset can gravely impact their productivity in a professional setting or their ability to pursue personal goals.

Prone to Procrastination

Procrastination and perfectionism go hand in hand. As we have discussed, perfectionists are inherently indecisive, which causes them to be stuck and unable to move forward, resulting in delayed growth and progress. Perfectionists feel anxiety and stress over the possibility of making mistakes, which often convinces them that putting things off until a later date is a good idea. This can make them miss out on good opportunities and be less productive at work, setting off a domino effect of negative impacts in their lives. If they can come to view making mistakes as an opportunity to try harder instead of being the end of the world, they will be able to remove this roadblock standing in their way and keeping them from reaching their goals.

We will unpack procrastination in the second part of this book.

Negative Effect on Relationships

As hard as perfectionists are on themselves, they are often equally hard on the people around them. They expect perfection and the achievement of impossibly high standards from everyone. When they inevitably don't get the perfect results they expect, they turn their very critical negative self-talk outward toward other people. They take out their stress, anxiety, and anger on others. That can make them very unpleasant and difficult, if not impossible, to be around. Critical and sometimes cruel comments directed toward the people around them are a recipe for harming relationships and decreasing the likelihood that healthy ones can be formed or maintained.

The Positive Sides of Perfectionism

We have discussed many of the negative side effects, but there are actually some positive results that can come from being a perfectionist. We have all heard the saying, "Everything in moderation." Well, perfectionism is no different. Having perfectionist tendencies can be good if they are kept in check and targeted toward just one area of your life. For example, Olympic athletes would not be able to achieve success at the pinnacle of their sport if they weren't relentless in their pursuit of excellence. We would expect them to be perfectionists when they train for and practice their sport. These athletes have to be committed to long and difficult training schedules often for years, at times be separated from their families, and perform well through injury and exhaustion. This would be impossible if they did not have intrinsic motivation. Perfectionism can certainly serve as that motivation to hone their skills and learn from their mistakes, fixing them to improve their athletic performance. In this case, when perfectionism is focused on one area, it can serve as the driving force to work harder, and make achieving their goals possible.

Athletes are not the only ones who can benefit from perfectionism when it is focused on only one area of life. People who are driven and focused on their careers can benefit as well if their perfectionist behaviors are kept in check and prevented from being taken to the extreme. In fact, most of us are glad that there are perfectionists out there, especially when it comes to how they help us. We want doctors, lawyers, pilots, teachers, and so many others to strive to be the best in their fields.

There is nothing inherently wrong with wanting to grow and improve or with the healthy pursuit of excellence. The key is for perfectionists to manage the degree to which perfectionism is an influence in their life, and how much of their life they allow it to touch—everything in moderation.

Key Takeaways:

- There is nothing wrong with setting high standards for yourself as long as they are not completely unrealistic and impossible to achieve, and you also recognize that those standards can often bring some negative consequences along with them.

- Perfectionists are often desire to receive approval from others. The problem comes when they rely on others for their sense of self-esteem. This, along with their often unrealistic expectations of others, can put a great deal of stress on their relationships and prevent them from forming or maintaining healthy ones.

- Perfectionism can hold people back and prevent them from being their best and living life to the fullest. It can act as a sort of mental paralysis. The fear of making the wrong choice or a mistake can prevent them from making any decision or being willing to take a risk. This keeps them from moving forward and causes them to miss out on opportunities for personal and professional growth and improvement.

- Perfectionism does not have to be all bad. If people are aware of their perfectionist tendencies and keep them in check, focused primarily on only one area of their life, they can serve as powerful motivation in the pursuit of excellence.

Chapter 3: Negative Side Effects of Perfectionism

Much like any medication you will ever take in your life, perfectionism comes with a whole boatload of unpleasant side effects. In the case of perfectionism, these negative side effects have the potential of having a profound and lasting impact on your life.

Success Doesn't Make You Happy

Successes are something to celebrate and enjoy. They represent goals achieved through hard work. You would think these accomplishments are reasons to be happy, but for the perfectionist mind, this is often not the case. Instead of congratulating themselves on a job well done, perfectionists often become fixated on one mistake or one thing that didn't go perfectly as planned. They can't let it go, and it ruins the happiness they could be enjoying. Examples of this can be found everywhere: the athlete who came in first place who is disappointed that they didn't break the record, the person who gave a well-received speech or presentation who is mad about the one point they forgot to mention in their delivery, the musician who played beautifully who is upset about playing one wrong note, the student who received an A on an exam who can't let go of the few questions she got wrong, or the chef who prepared a delicious meal who is frustrated that he left out one ingredient.

Perfectionists focus on their perceived failures instead of their successes. They expect success and in fact demand it from themselves, so they ignore that and fixate on their mistakes and the things that went wrong. They turn to inward criticism, which robs them of the happiness they should be enjoying.

Becoming Defensive, and an Inability to Consider Constructive Criticism

While perfectionists are experts at criticizing themselves, they are still human, which means they do not relish receiving criticism from others. They take it to heart and take it personally, often becoming very defensive and trying to blame other people or circumstances for why they didn't achieve the expected results. In essence, because their sense of self-worth is so tied to the opinions that others have of them, they are afraid that people are seeing all of their imperfections, so they try to distract and deflect their attention elsewhere. They see it as a means of self-preservation.

Not Asking for Help, with a Wish to Retain Control

Perfectionists fear the unknown. Unpredictable things are a great source of anxiety for them. They like things to be done a certain way and assume if they want things done right, they should do it themselves. Perfectionists crave control because without it they feel defenseless and susceptible to failure. When perfectionists do allow others to do some of the work, they still are unwilling to relinquish complete control. They stand by them watching their every move, trying to ensure that mistakes are not made so that perfection can be achieved. This causes low morale in the people they work with as they feel resentful of the perfectionist's lack of trust in them. This may make a perfectionist very difficult and unpleasant to work with and causes an unproductive and unhealthy workplace environment.

Perfectionists aren't alone in being resistant to ask for help. The problem is that, as with most things, perfectionists take this to the extreme. They think that if they ask for help they are revealing inadequacies and showing weakness; if they can't do things all by themselves, it equals failure. They feel guilt and shame if they have to ask others for help. Since they see things as black and white—successes or failures—with no room for anything else in between, they view seeking help as an ultimate failure. They want to appear perfect to those around them, so they are willing to struggle and work for hours on a problem that could often be resolved much more quickly if they were willing to reach out to ask for help.

As we have discussed, perfectionists crave control. There are many reasons for this. If they hand over control to others, they imagine an array of horrible things as being likely to happen. First, they think that they are more susceptible to failure by trusting someone else to do something they feel they are better equipped to handle on their own. Second, perfectionists like to show off their knowledge and skills to others—this is where they get their feeling of self-worth. By giving away their control to others, they think it makes them look less important and less of a critical component of success. Perfectionism sometimes pushes people to be more proud than humble and to not want to risk having others look better than they do.

Recovery from Mistakes and Failures Becomes Difficult

Mistakes are learning opportunities which can help us to grow. When we make mistakes, we become problem solvers and better critical thinkers as we seek to do better in the future. Unfortunately, perfectionists don't view mistakes that way. They fixate on them and beat themselves up. They criticize themselves and can't let go of it and move on. They view mistakes as failures that can't be forgiven. It doesn't matter whether the mistake is big or small, or made by themselves or others. Mistakes are all viewed in the same way. Most perfectionists aren't known for giving themselves or others second chances. In their mind, if someone fails to meet their unrealistically high standards, an imprint has been made and they have a very hard time letting that go and moving forward.

Analysis Paralysis, or Difficulty Finishing Things

Perfectionists will often put off making a decision in order to avoid making the "wrong" one, and do not realize that is a choice as well. Perfectionists are happy to make decisions when they consider them as being in an area of their strengths, but they will avoid making a decision or taking a risk in weaker areas.

This causes perfectionists to react to risks or making decisions in one of two ways. Either they avoid making any decision or taking any action at all, essentially remaining stuck in quicksand and unable to grow as they refuse to push themselves beyond their comfort zone. Or they enter a state of "analysis paralysis." This is where they continue to seek information thinking that if they only have every piece of information available they will be able to make an informed decision. They continue to analyze and re-analyze the pros and cons of every potential risk or decision and can't bring themselves to take a stand and move forward.

We all have heard of Steve Jobs, the genius behind so many of the products at Apple who contributed to our lives through technology in probably more ways than we can count. He is a well-known perfectionist who expected perfection from both himself and others in the workplace. But he suffered from analysis paralysis in his personal life as well. He once shared a story illustrating how his perfectionism impacted even very routine decisions in his life.

His family was considering buying a new washing machine and his perfectionist tendencies went into overdrive. He recalled the decision-making process they went through. He wanted to analyze every aspect of the washing machine before purchasing one. He thoroughly studied the design of many models and spoke with his family about what was most important in their house, like the amount of time it would take to wash a load of laundry, the gentleness of the machine on their clothes in terms of them remaining soft and lasting longer, or how much water the washing machine used. Steve Jobs spent two weeks discussing this with his family every night over dinner before ultimately making a decision. This is a perfect example of analysis paralysis.

Higher Risk of Depression[i]

Thinking that the only acceptable outcome is perfection and the constant need to live up to impossibly high standards wears away at perfectionists over time. All of the stress and anxiety can take their toll and put them at a greater risk for experiencing depression. Kenneth G. Rice, PhD, a psychology professor from the University of Florida, conducted a study published in the *Journal of Counseling Psychology*. He studied eighty-four college students over the span of fifteen weeks during which he gave them psychological assessment scales to evaluate their levels of perfectionism and depression. He found that the students who exhibited characteristics of maladaptive perfectionism had a high correlation with depression, while those students who exhibited characteristics of adaptive perfectionism, in which they had very high standards and the pursuit of excellence without as much self-criticism, did not have a connection to depression.[ii]

Key Takeaways:

- Perfectionism goes hand in hand with many negative side effects that can impact your life in countless ways.

- Perfectionists tend to focus on the negatives and what went wrong instead of being able to celebrate and enjoy their successes.

- Perfectionists can have a hard time working with others. They often get defensive when they think anyone is being critical of them and often try to place the blame on other people or circumstances in order to deflect attention from imperfections. They have a hard time delegating or relinquishing control and see asking for help as a sign of weakness.

- Perfectionism can make people unable to learn from mistakes and grow as they are afraid to push themselves beyond their comfort zone. They view mistakes as failures and they fixate on them, unable to let them go.

- People who are perfectionists can suffer from analysis paralysis, where they refuse to take risks or make decisions for fear of making the wrong choice. All of the constant stress and anxiety can also make maladaptive perfectionists more susceptible to depression.

Chapter 4: How to Overcome Perfectionist Habits

Now that we have learned about the many negative side effects accompanying perfectionism, it's time to learn how to overcome or keep them in check. This chapter will lay out strategies that you can begin to put to work in your life today.

Imperfection Doesn't Equal Failure

The first step in breaking free of all of the stress, guilt, and disappointment you feel when unrealistically high standards aren't met is to accept that the perfection you have been chasing isn't based on anything more than an illusion. The main problem surrounding perfectionism is that it is celebrated in our culture. Children are encouraged to get the perfect score on tests to get the perfect job and have the perfect life. It never works that way, but that's the projected image.

Let's break that myth. Think back on a time when you did achieve a perfect score on a test, delivered a perfect presentation, or did something else flawlessly. How did it affect your life? Did it make a major impact on your career or life in general? Probably not. Perfection is not necessary for any of the things we are pursuing.

Gaining awareness of this fact and accepting it as true, therefore, is the first step in turning that perfect ship around. As a practice, try to recall three things you think you did without erring. Whatever it was. Write them down.

1.

2.

3.

Now try to recall how much work and time it cost you to achieve that result.

1.

2.

3.

Finally, assess how this accomplishment affected your life five minutes later, one day later, one year later, and ten years later. Maybe delivering the perfect speech earned you some recognition, some approving nods from your superiors. Maybe the next day some people still recalled your exceptional performance and gave you a pat on the back. But no one admired you for the speech one or ten years later, right? Think about what you had to sacrifice for it. A month's worth of play time with your kids in the evening? Four date nights with your partner? Important time for self-care?

What would have happened if you delivered a speech just eighty percent as good as the original? How much more time and energy could you have spent on different things in life? Everything we choose to has a trade-off; if we invest our time playing the piano, we won't be able to go fishing. If we buy a PS5, we won't be able to buy a new fridge. If we deliver the perfect speech, we trade off being a better parent, partner, or child.

The second thing we need to assess is how much of our perfectionism is driven by a thirst for control. As much as we'd like to think otherwise, it is impossible to control everything. In fact, if we took the time to stop and think about all of the things that happen in our day that are beyond our control, it might be alarming. From the rain that inevitably popped up just as we were leaving the grocery store, to the surprise new project that was sprung on us at work, to the car that pulls out right in front of us, there are many things that we will never be able to control, try as we might. That's not to say that we can't be smart and attempt to prepare ourselves to better handle the unexpected events life throws our way, but we must also acknowledge our own limitations when it comes to our ability to control everything.

A perfectionist's mind wants the scoreboard of life to display their name with a very high number of points, and their mistakes at zero.

Mistakes will happen throughout your entire life. It's the way of the world, and you might as well just go along for the ride and accept it. They are like the spices we add to our cooking. Mistakes are what give our lives flavor. Granted, the initial taste may not always be immediately pleasing to the palate, but it will build character and give us the best stories to tell later in life. Mistakes are a bit like vegetables: they may not be what we want to reach for first in the feast of life, but they are good for us and help us to grow.

Think about three things that you want to be perfect in out of a thirst for control. Then consider why. For example, you noticed that sometimes when you go out with friends to eat, your hands start to shake and the food either skips off your spoon or your plate and the utensils make a rhythmic, clattering sound. You hate this habit of yours, as you consider it a telltale sign of social anxiety, and that is a sign of weakness which can't be shown. It does not fit with the personality you want to project. Thus, you either never order food, saying you're not hungry, or you avoid social settings in a restaurant.

What would be so terrible in showing some anxiety? What if people would accept you like that? Now, back to our task: Name three things you wish to control perfectly in your life. What is the reason behind it? What outcome do you dread?

1.

2.

3.

Allow Yourself to Be Wrong, to Make Mistakes

This sounds like an easy proposition, but mistakes strike fear in the heart of anyone. They are the visible proof of (perceived) inadequacy. When they make mistakes, a perfectionist's ever-critical inner voice starts working to point out all of the ways that they have failed, which makes them feel guilty and ashamed, like they have let themselves and others down and should have done better.

The irony is that it is in making mistakes that we can ever hope to grow and improve. Perfectionists see mistakes as an outcome or ending. They can't move forward. They just keep spinning their wheels in the mud.

My mom was an example in how mistakes can help you to learn, grow, and achieve something even better than you had hoped for. My dad loved food. In particular, he loved his mother's cooking. When my parents got married, my dad asked my mom to prepare some of his favorite dishes just like his mother had. The problem was that my grandmother wasn't exactly the best at writing down her recipes for others to follow. When my mom went to her for guidance, she would say things like use a pinch of this or that ingredient. My mom didn't let that deter her. She tried to make my grandmother's oyster dressing every Thanksgiving and Christmas, getting feedback from my dad all along the way. Sometimes the attempt was so bad that it would get thrown out, and sometimes it was very close. My mom could have easily gotten discouraged and beaten herself up over it or given up completely, but she didn't. She just kept making notes on her recipe cards vowing to make it better the next time.

When I was eight years old, my mom made oyster dressing so good that my dad declared it tasted just like his mom's, and in fact was even an improvement on the recipe. My grandma agreed. Sadly, we lost my grandmother the following year, but her recipe with my mom's improvements has now been passed on to future generations. I'm so glad that my mom viewed her mistakes as opportunities to learn, grow, and improve. She saw each one as a tool that could teach her something and, as a result, she created something even better that she ever hoped for.

Take a moment to think of something you have been avoiding doing out of fear that you will make a mistake. List all of the things you are afraid might go wrong.

Now, for each one ask yourself, "So what?" Envision the worst possible scenario that might go wrong in each instance. You might be surprised to find that even if the worst happened in every single one of your worries, it isn't going to be as bad as you had built it up in your mind to be. While Murphy's Law does seem to rear its ugly head in our lives at times, it is very rare that the worst-case scenario ever comes true—especially not every single time.

Taking the time to write down your fears of making mistakes can help you to see that things are unlikely to turn out as badly as you worry they might. You can isolate the fears that are holding you back and begin to overcome them and move forward, less anxious and more confident.

Do this exercise:

1. Write down four major perfectionism-driven fears and problems you've been putting off to overcome. They can be any kind of fear, from overcoming

public anxiety to dating struggles. Done? Let's go to step two.

2. Look at each of your choices and ask yourself: Why have you delayed taking action to solve them? What pain are you trying to save yourself from by not taking action? For example, in the case of practicing public speaking, it would be too painful to humiliate yourself in front of people while practicing, so you would rather not improve it at all to avoid the perceived humiliation. You save yourself from temporary discomfort, but in the long run it will bring you more sorrow to your life, which takes us to step 3.

3. Write down what you will miss out on by not taking action. In the case of

public speaking, if you don't improve this skill you may never be able to deliver your message to people properly. If you work in sales or marketing this can have a severe effect on your chances of getting promoted. Promotion for perfectionists is like winning the gold medal. What chances will you miss? Say it out loud, "I will lose money," "I will miss the promotion," "I won't maximize my potential as a salesperson."

4. The last step of this exercise is to write down what you will gain if you focus on the long-term benefits of overcoming a perfectionism-related fear. For example, "By improving my public speaking I will get more confident about this skill. I won't have any more sleepless nights, I can sell my products more

convincingly, I will be able to make more money …" Collect all the benefits you'd get from defeating a perfectionist habit or fear.

No one likes to be wrong. Our brains are hardwired to always want to be right, so admitting that we are wrong doesn't come easily or naturally to us. It is something that takes time and effort on our part. But we are human—we make mistakes. We do the best we can with what we have at the time, and when we know better we do better. We are all deeply invested in our ideas, opinions, and the actions we take in our lives. But these should not be viewed as permanent. After all, we are works in progress—living, growing, changing beings—and our ideas, opinions, and actions change along with us if we receive information that warrants it.

Being wrong doesn't diminish our worth. It just means that in light of new information, our opinion is no longer accurate, or our actions can be improved upon. In fact, being humble enough to recognize our mistake and try better is proof of great character.

When we make mistakes, most of the time people don't realize them unless we point them out. If they do notice, they think of them as no big deal. While we are stressing out and assuming that everyone is thinking the worst of us, most of the time they either aren't paying attention or they think the mistakes are minor, and that we will fix them. They don't think that we aren't skilled at what we do. They don't spend nearly the amount of time judging us as we do ourselves.

Lower Unreasonably High Standards and Expectations

The way to silence your critical inner voice that chips away at your self-esteem is to change your standards and expectations so that they are based in reality and stand a fighting chance of being achieved.

Ask yourself what you would like to accomplish today. Write everything down. You probably hate writing stuff down. I used to hate it, too. Every time I read a book on self-help and the author said "now take a pen and paper and write down …" I felt betrayed. "Why? Why do I need to write? Isn't it enough if I just think about it?" The problem is that if I wouldn't give this speech on the importance of writing right now, you'd probably be on the next page already, not even thinking about your daily accomplishments. When you get to the end of the book you'd think, "Oh, there were some nuggets here and there, but I didn't get to know much about myself or how to solve my problems." I don't want you to think that. I want you to feel successful and full of ideas on how to improve yourself. But you won't get there unless you stop for a moment and write things down. Why? Because:

- By writing, you disconnect from the book and you enter the realm of your thoughts. You'll stop and think about parts of your life you normally don't. You'll discover new parts of your day, your personality.
- Written things are more likely to stick. While thoughts fly away, the action of writing makes a greater impact on you, especially if you don't write things down very often.

- Written things are traceable. For example, five years ago I made some notes on my thoughts following my re-reading of a book. A few weeks ago, I found and read my notes and I was astonished about how many things came true that I wished for five years ago. It's mind blowing ... Please take the paper and pen, do your future self a favor, and write down your precious thoughts. You'll love yourself for it.

Okay, back to the exercise. Write down what you wish to accomplish today. Then write down what success looks like to you for each goal on your list. This may be difficult or seem unimportant, but it really is—especially if you want to break free of a perfectionist cycle.

1.

2.

3.

We are doing ourselves a disservice if we don't spell out our standards for success clearly in advance. We may not even consciously think of them until we are judging ourselves against them to determine if we were a success or failure. Then our negative, critical inner voice has a heyday pointing out all of our mistakes and flaws. That's not fair. That would be like us going to the DMV to take our driving test without knowing what we would need to do to pass it, and then hearing in the end that we failed. They say sunshine is the best disinfectant, so get those standards out in writing where they can be seen.

Once you have your standards for success written out in front of you, take a good hard look at them. Ask yourself if they are realistic. You can play an imaginary movie in your head looking at yourself executing your task as you planned it. Was it a good movie? If yes, your expectation is just as unrealistic as movie scenes. The majority of our tasks, if we keep them real, wouldn't make a good movie scene. Think about them again and try to simplify them. Before you invest too much effort in the simplification, think about whether they are really important to you or not.

Decide if the investment of time and energy required to meet your standard of success is worth it in the long run. Then adjust your standards. Lower them enough so that they are achievable. You'll find that in the end you get a lot more accomplished than you otherwise would have because you won't feel the need to put things off because you are paralyzed by the fear of making a mistake. You'll find that your inner critic has a lot less to say when you have realistic standards.

Our standards are the goals we set for ourselves. They are the bar we think we need to reach, and we won't be satisfied with our performance if it is anything less. Like hurdles in a race—if runners don't clear the hurdle, their time is slowed and they aren't pleased with their performance.

Our standards work in the same way for us. They can (and should) be high, but keeping them realistic and attainable is key. Our expectations are what we believe should happen if we reach our standards. In our running analogy, if our standard is that we clear all of the hurdles, our expectation might be that we win the race, or that we run it under a certain amount of time. The problem with our expectations is that they often depend on a number of variables that are beyond our control. For example, in our race the weather and the condition of the track could easily play a role in how fast we run or whether or not we win. If it is raining or windy our pace will be slowed down. If the track is slippery, or not in good condition, adjusting our speed may be necessary. If a competitor pushes in our lane causing us to fall, or there is a problem with our shoe, the outcome can be very different than what our expectations were. That's just life. Many things beyond our control can impact our expectations.

Perfectionists usually can't separate the things beyond their control from themselves in their minds. They see not meeting their standards and expectations as a failure on their part, no matter the cause. They blame themselves.

Just like you did earlier with your standards, take a minute to write down your expectations about a standard you have set for yourself. Remember the power of putting them in writing so you can see them.

1.

2.

3.

Adjusting your expectations to reflect what is within your control makes them reasonable and attainable. You can avoid setting yourself up for unnecessary disappointment before you even start, and give yourself a fighting chance to meet or even exceed your expectations, all the while keeping your perfectionist tendencies in check.

Sheldon Cooper, a character on the television show *The Big Bang Theory*, played by Jim Parsons, displays many perfectionist tendencies, not the least of which is his impossibly high standards and expectations. One example of this is his insistence in always sitting in the same seat in his apartment. He explains that his seat is perfect because in the winter it is close enough to the radiator that it keeps him warm, but not too close that it makes him sweat. In the summer, it's in the perfect spot to feel the breeze through the windows and is perfectly positioned to see the television while still being able to carry on conversations with people in the room. That's a lot of pressure to put on a spot on the couch. Sheldon might benefit from adjusting the expectations he has for sitting in his seat and realizing that there are many things beyond his control, such as the breeze coming in the window, the amount of heat coming out of the radiator, the location of the television and other furniture, and whether new ones might ever be purchased, and the inevitable frustration and stress he feels when others enter his apartment and attempt to sit in his spot.

Monica Geller, another famous television character on the television show *Friends*, played by Courtney Cox, is an excellent example of a perfectionist who could benefit from making her standards and expectations more realistic and attainable. She likes to be extremely organized and clean, and holds herself and her friends to those impossibly high standards. She is addicted to her label maker and has binders and lists for everything, doesn't like to let others touch her binders without washing their hands first, is afraid to let people look at her photos because they will get smudges and fingerprints all over them, and nearly passed out when someone dropped and broke one of her plates. She was accused of cleaning her toilet seventeen times a day, even when people were on it, and admitted to cleaning in her sleep. Monica's perfectionism must be exhausting!

Explore outside of Your Comfort Zone and Try Something New That You Are Unskilled In

Perfectionists see themselves as experts in their comfort zones. As a result, they consistently set impossibly high, unrealistic expectations for themselves. Since they are human, mistakes will happen. When they don't meet their standards and expectations their inner critic goes to work as they are hard on themselves. Perfectionists stay stuck in this never-ending cycle because they assume that if things go wrong in areas that they have expertise in, they should never try new things because failure will be inevitable.

People need to expand their comfort zones if they ever hope to break free of the cycle. It isn't easy and it takes time and effort. A good place to start is to make a list of ten things that you can see as being worthwhile to do but that make you feel nervous or uncomfortable. These might be initiating a conversation at work with a boss or coworker you don't know very well, hosting a dinner party at your house, taking an art class, writing a book, exercising at the gym, calling an old friend or family member who you lost touch with, or traveling to a foreign country.

1.

2.

3.

4.

5.

6.

7.

8.

9.

10.

On this list, beside each item, write down the worst possible thing you can imagine happening if you were to do it. By putting your worries in writing, you are taking away the power they hold over you. You are acknowledging that, while things may not turn out perfectly, they probably won't be as bad as you imagined and you will survive (and quite possibly grow) during the process.

Doing something new that one is unskilled in strikes fear. Perfectionists are afraid to look silly. Well, they are partially right. When we try something new, we are likely to make mistakes. Helen Hayes wisely said, "An expert at anything was once a beginner." Mistakes aren't proof that we don't measure up. They are just learning opportunities. They teach us what worked and what didn't, and show us how we can improve in the future. When we acknowledge that, yes, we are probably going to make mistakes, we take away their power. We give ourselves the permission and freedom to make them without allowing our critical inner voice to judge us too harshly. We realize that mistakes aren't the end of the world. Most of the time they are no big deal. We can learn from them and move on.

Go back to your list of worthwhile things that make you nervous or uncomfortable. Ask yourself what some mistakes that you might make in each one are. Then figure out how you might go about fixing and overcoming those mistakes.

Take traveling to a foreign country, for example. You might make mistakes in speaking an unfamiliar language. How might you go about fixing that? You might try to take a course in the language before your trip. You might speak to people you know who have travelled there before or research online for advice. You might take along a translation dictionary or try to find someone who speaks English to help you. By understanding that mistakes can be learned from, corrected, and overcome, you remove some of the fear that comes with trying new things.

Reframe Your Thoughts on Criticism

Our human nature is to defend ourselves when we receive criticism from others. Even on our best days, when we can objectively see that there is some merit to the criticism we receive, we are still likely to justify to others why we did what we did. It's just the way our brains are wired. Accepting criticism graciously, and even welcoming it, is not something that comes easily and naturally to us.

Perfectionists take criticism very personally. They instantly feel a lot of negative emotions and are both mad at themselves and the person giving them criticism. They are afraid that others will think poorly of them. They feel anxious thinking they have let people down and should have done better. They see it as proof that they aren't good enough. They see themselves as a failure, and are unable to recognize that when someone gives them constructive criticism they are coming from a good place. People who have constructive criticism have seen an area that can be improved upon and want to help them fix it for the future. Constructive criticism can help to point out things that we may not realize about ourselves, allowing us to learn and grow from it.

Think about the last time you received constructive criticism. Ask yourself the following questions:

- Were they trying to help me?
- Were the statements they made about my performance accurate?
- If I took their advice, how might my performance improve?
- Did I think my performance was perfect before they said anything?

By doing this, you are looking at the criticism through a constructive lens. You are keeping negative feelings such as anger and defensiveness in check as you look at the criticism for what it really is: feedback that you alone can decide whether you should take it or leave it.

Set Strict Deadlines

Parkinson's Law states that work will expand to fill up the amount of time you have to complete it. If I tell my kids that they have an hour to clean up their rooms, it will take them at least an hour to do it. If my wife knows she has two days to get ready for vacation, she will use the full two days. As a teacher, I found that if I did not set and stick to strict deadlines with some of my students, they were content to spend the entire school day working on an assignment that should have taken them twenty minutes. However, if I set a timer for those students, they were much more likely to be more productive and get the work completed in the allotted time and sometimes even more quickly than I expected.

When given a choice, perfectionists would prefer to work on a project until it is perfect. This is true of any project, as they do not naturally make distinctions about when "good enough" is just fine. If perfectionists set strict deadlines for themselves, they have to commit to walking away when the time is up, even if their work isn't perfect. Otherwise, they would happily continue making improvements to their work indefinitely. In theory, there is nothing wrong with that and it can even be an admirable trait, but every project reaches a point when continued improvements make a very minor difference, if any at all. Concentrate on finishing your work instead of perfecting it.

There is a famous quote: "Don't let the perfect be the enemy of the good." This is a constant struggle for perfectionists. One way to start to overcome this tendency is to think about something that you take great pride in doing perfectly and note how long it usually takes you to do it. Then set the timer for substantially less time and challenge yourself to see how much you can get done. You should be more efficient with your time since you don't have a moment to waste. You won't have time to get bogged down in the minute details of wanting to be perfect. You will understand that perfection isn't your goal. It won't be possible.

All you can do is the absolute best job you can in the time you have been given. Then you have to walk away. In time, with practice, you will find yourself wanting to apply this in more and more areas of your life. It won't be easy, but eventually it will become more like second nature.

Key Takeaways:

- Perfectionist tendencies are present within all of us to varying degrees, and will take time, effort, practice, and commitment to overcome.

- Perfection is an illusion that doesn't truly exist. The relentless pursuit of it will lead to exhaustion, frustration, disappointment, guilt, and shame and can cause unintended negative consequences in our personal and professional lives.

- You can quiet the overly critical inner voice within you by giving yourself permission to make mistakes and be wrong.

- Lower your standards and expectations to make them realistic and attainable.

Take into account there are some influences beyond your control; this will help lower your stress and anxiety levels and increase your self-esteem.

- Recognizing that no one focuses as much as you do on your mistakes because everyone has their own issues and problems to deal with can be a very liberating experience.

- Expanding your comfort zone by being willing to try new things without fear of making mistakes, and being open to objectively evaluating the constructive criticism from others, offers opportunities for learning and growth.

- Focus on finishing your work, not perfecting it.

Chapter 5: How to Heal the Perfectionist Soul

Cultivate Authenticity: Let Go of What People Think

If you stood on a busy sidewalk and questioned people walking by about the kinds of qualities they value in others, you would get responses like honest, trustworthy, kind, genuine, down-to-earth, straightforward, helpful, and generous. These are all wonderful characteristics worthy of admiration. Chances are, these are the same qualities that all of us would like to find in ourselves, too. While the genes we were born with and the way that we were raised influence the kind of person we become and the way others describe us, our characteristics do not have to be set in stone. We are intelligent human beings who can make choices of our own free will every day that help to determine the kind of people we are.

In her book, *The Gifts of Imperfection*, Brene Brown has done extensive research on perfectionism and authenticity. She thinks most people consider authenticity as a quality that people either have or they don't. She once believed that herself but has since changed her mind. Brown refers to authenticity as "a practice—a conscious choice of how we want to live. Authenticity is a collection of choices we have to make every day. It's about the choice to show up and be real. The choice to be honest; to let our true selves be seen." She admits that being authentic is something that some people choose to practice, something that some people don't, and something that some people do the best they can, but they still have their successful and unsuccessful days at trying to achieve.

We are products of a society where we are encouraged to please others and seek their approval. Pop culture sets the trends that are valued in everything—clothing, our physical appearance, the kind of car we drive, the desirable neighborhoods to live in, the types of schools we should attend, and even how we raise our children. If we want to keep up with the Joneses and fit in, authenticity doesn't come easily since we have an image to protect. Sometimes this may mean that we make the choice to go along with the crowd, or do and say things to try to make ourselves appear better than we really are. It may mean that we only let people get so close to us and we keep some parts of our lives hidden from others, because we don't want them to see that we aren't really perfect.

Brown believes that people are authentic when they let go of their image of who they think they should be and celebrate who they really are—imperfections and all. They choose to allow others to see them as they are and don't try to act like someone they aren't. When they choose to be authentic, they are brave enough to be themselves around others and risk being judged while not being too hard on themselves when they make mistakes. They are kind and understanding toward others, and build strong, honest relationships because they feel like they are on an equal footing with those around them, rather than feeling as though they don't measure up. To be truly authentic, we have to practice it in both good and difficult times and be willing to experience all of the emotions that go along with it.

Shakespeare summed up the importance of being authentic in his famous quote from Hamlet: "This above all to thine own self be true." Perfectionists may find it a scary proposition to be authentic and reveal their imperfections, as it can leave them feeling very open and vulnerable to criticism. But if they can recognize the value in not having to put on a performance in an attempt to maintain a perfect façade, they might find life to be a lot less stressful and more healing for the soul. As with most of the strategies we have discussed in this book to help us overcome our perfectionist tendencies, it is easier said than done and requires effort, commitment, and practice on our part to make it happen.

In *The Gifts of Imperfection,* Brown reminds us of the possibility that our new attempts at living a more authentic life may not always be well-received by others. We may hit some rough patches as we change the way that we have previously related to others. Some people in our lives will welcome and applaud our efforts, while others may be resistant to any kind of change that they aren't used to. We might experience regret at rocking the boat and speaking our mind because we may find others whispering about us behind our backs, or wondering if others think of us differently now. We will likely worry that others will not like our new more authentic selves as much as they like the perfect façade we previously shared with the world. Doubts will certainly creep in from time to time and tempt us to turn back to our old ways. We may fear that by speaking out we may hurt the feelings of others, or make them feel like we are showing off or that we think we are somehow smarter or better than them.[iii]

Most of us were taught and encouraged to be people-pleasers. This doesn't necessarily have to be a bad thing, as long as it isn't at the expense of having our own identity and self-esteem. Moving toward living a more authentic life is a paradigm shift in that we will have to focus on ourselves—our thoughts, opinions, and needs—at times. This may feel uncomfortable for many people, especially at first. It may help to think of the safety presentations given on airlines where we are told to put the oxygen masks on ourselves before we try to help others. It may go against our first instinct as we always want to help those we care about, but we won't be able to help anyone if we don't take care of ourselves first.

Showing your true unvarnished self to others is risky. It opens you up to people who criticize others not to build them up and help them improve, but because tearing people down somehow makes them feel better about themselves. As we have discussed before, receiving criticism is never easy. It goes against our human nature and doesn't feel good. It is tempting to want to tune out any and all criticism and build up our walls so that we don't get hurt, but we might miss out on some wonderful relationships and some great joys in life.

The secret is to look at criticism objectively to see if it comes from a good place, from someone who cares about us and genuinely wants to help, or if it comes from someone who is intentionally trying to be hurtful and cruel. Then we analyze the criticism to see if it has merit or not. If it does, we find a way to use it to our benefit and learn and grow from it. If it doesn't, we have to find a way to let it go and move forward without dwelling on it and beating ourselves up over it. This isn't an easy thing to do, but it is absolutely necessary for our own well-being.

Moving toward living a more authentic life is an adjustment, and it will take some time for everyone to get used to the changes in relationships and their dynamics. Think of it as sharing your true self with the world. It is a gift to yourself because you are taking away all of the stress and pressure you put on yourself trying to keep up a perfect façade and just being you. It is a gift to others because, now that you aren't so consumed with trying to please everyone all of the time, you can focus your time and attention on building stronger relationships with those you love the most.

Brown puts it in perspective by pointing out that if your goal is to be liked, accepted, and approved of by everyone, you are setting yourself up for failure because that is impossible and will never happen. You will be left feeling frustration, disappointment, and you eill even blame yourself. But if your goal is to be authentic and your true self, you will be better prepared to deal with it if others don't like or accept you for who you really are. People will either come around or they won't, but either way, we will come through the other side stronger for it. It won't be easy, but it will be worth it.

We want to live a more authentic life, but how do we go about achieving it? Keep in mind that try as we might, the road to living authentically will not be a completely smooth one. Even with our best efforts and intentions, there are bound to be setbacks and bumps in the road. We all have our moments when we allow self-doubt to creep in, and we find ourselves in situations where we wonder if being our true selves is good enough, or suitable in certain situations or environments. It is then that we may find ourselves retreating into our shells a bit and feeling more at ease trying to be the version of ourselves that we think everyone will like or approve of, rather than being comfortable in our own skin and sharing who we truly are. The following tips may prove helpful in your quest toward a life with greater authenticity:

- Get to know yourself. Try to pay special attention to the way you act and feel in different areas of your life. Where are you the most comfortable? Where are you nervous? Are there people and situations where you feel the most free to be yourself? Are there any certain triggers you can start to recognize where you find yourself feeling like a fish out of water—wishing you could be someone or someplace else? The more aware you are of yourself and your feelings, the more you will be able to redirect yourself if you start to try to hide your authentic self. You will know your strengths and weaknesses and easily recognize when you are acting in a way that doesn't fit with your values and beliefs. This enables you to quickly change course when necessary and get back to the core of who you are.

- Get to know the people around you. How many times do you say hi to someone and ask them how they are without really hearing the answer? I gave my students the same writing prompt on the first day of school every year: "I really wish my teacher knew…" The answers I would get were pretty amazing. They wanted to open up and tell me about themselves—they just didn't always realize it. By asking them about themselves, I created a bond with them where they trusted me. I always opened up a bit with them in return. They felt valued and heard and liked that I trusted them, too. It created an instant connection and got our school year and new relationships off to a great start. If you take the time to really listen to and get to know the people around you, you will go a long way toward being more genuine and down-to-earth—not to mention forming some pretty great relationships along the way.

- Live in the moment. Be present. Authentic people give others the attention they deserve. How many times have you sat down to play a game with your kids, but your mind was elsewhere thinking of all the things you needed to get done? Or you were talking to a friend or colleague but you didn't really hear a word they said because you were too busy trying to come up with the perfect way to respond? Being present in the moment and really listening to others is one of the most authentic things you can do.

- Examine the things that you care about. See if the values and beliefs you once held are still important to you in your life today. You are a living, growing being who is constantly changing. The things you hold dear should be allowed to evolve with you. Authentic people check in periodically on the things that are important to them to be sure they are still a good fit with the person they are today.

- Don't waste valuable time trying to be perfect. As we've discussed, perfection is an illusion—that mirage in the desert which only really exists in your mind, which is futile to chase and will always be beyond your reach. A good first step is to shake your perfectionist tendency of thinking that things are black or white, right or wrong, perfect or a failure. Embrace life and all it has to offer. Be open-minded and receptive to different people and viewpoints. See the world through a lens which allows you to appreciate not only black and white but also every shade of gray in between. Be proud of who you are—flaws and all. You'll find that it makes you mush more likeable, approachable, and relatable to others.

Cultivate Self-Compassion: You Are Enough

All too often perfectionism and feeling ashamed go hand in hand. We think that if only we can be perfect in all areas of our life, we won't ever have to be judged critically by ourselves or others and experience the feeling of pain and rejection that goes along with it. We think that being perfect will protect us, when in reality it is the anchor weighing us down and keeping us from reaching our full potential. We become so consumed with how we think others see us and gaining their approval that we end up losing our sense of self in the process. We are so afraid of making mistakes, failing, and disappointing others that we avoid trying new things and taking risks. This causes us to get stuck in a rut and be unable to learn from our mistakes and grow. We end up missing out on many of the wonderful opportunities and joy that life has to offer. It becomes a cycle that can be very difficult to break.

Everyone has perfectionist tendencies within them to varying degrees. Some people may only seek perfection in times when they are feeling vulnerable, while others seem to be addicted to it so much that it can become all-consuming and impact their lives in countless negative ways. In order to begin to overcome our perfectionist tendencies in any degree, it is imperative to be more compassionate toward ourselves. Facing our fears and changing our critical inner voice are important first steps toward embracing our imperfections and breaking free of the perfectionist cycle.[iv]

The critical inner voice of perfectionists blames them for all of their shortcomings and flaws. It makes them feel like they aren't good enough or deserving of the love of others, or that they're ever going to be accepted and fit in unless they change and achieve perfection. It is important to reframe this voice and make it more positive. Our inner voice should ideally be telling us that who we are is enough and any changes and improvements we aspire to make should be because we want to make them for ourselves—not to win the acceptance and approval of others.

That paradigm shift is key, as we should know and acknowledge our imperfections without being consumed with or ashamed of them. We need to show ourselves some patience and compassion rather than being so eager to judge ourselves harshly. When we are compassionate toward ourselves, we acknowledge our feelings and address them without being too hard on ourselves, or fixating on them too much or for too long. We recognize that it is human nature to feel as though we don't measure up to others at times and we are not alone in experiencing those feelings. Brown shared a line from Leonard Cohen's song "Anthem" that sums up why we should show ourselves some compassion: "There is a crack in everything. That's how the light gets in." Sometimes it helps to remember that we are all perfectly imperfect.

How do we go about showing ourselves more compassion? Here are some tips that can set you on the path toward giving yourself a little more TLC (tender loving care):

- Show yourself the same kindness that you would show the most vulnerable people you love. Think of how you would react if your child (or any child) came to you because they were hurt, afraid or upset. You would likely be very calm, gentle, and compassionate. Or think of your beloved pet, cherished friend, or an elderly parent—you would want to comfort them and help to make their pain go away. Practice showing yourself the same tenderness and compassion as you would show the people you love the most.

- Be mindful and present in the moment. The times when we are the hardest on ourselves are often when we get stuck in our heads and keep stewing over something that went badly. Our overly critical inner voice runs rampant and we tend to replay the negative feelings over and over in our mind to the point where it is difficult to move past it. Being mindful can help us snap out of it and stay focused on the moment at hand rather than judging ourselves too harshly.

- Remember that you're human. There are roughly 7.5 billion of us on the planet, give or take several million, and there is a lot more that unites us than divides us. One of the most important traits we all have in common is that none of us are perfect. So take it easy on yourself! We're all in the same boat!

- Look at your mistakes as a blip on the radar or a bump in the road. We all make them and it's not the end of the world. Making a mistake doesn't define who you are. It was just a moment in time.

Pick yourself up, dust yourself off, and keep moving forward.

- Don't be afraid to lean on your support system. This self-compassion doesn't come easily. It takes effort and practice and invariably we will slip up. It's ok to rely on others for support. They can help you keep things in perspective and show you compassion and empathy when you need it the most. They can remind you of your good qualities and offer levity. Your support system may come in the form of friends or family members or even a therapist or life coach. The only requirement is that they are there for you and can help keep you grounded when you are tempted to let your critical inner voice take over.

Let Go of the Need for Certainty

We've talked a lot about our critical inner voice, but that isn't the only voice at work inside us. Our intuition is with us as well, but it doesn't always command the same attention. Our intuition, or gut feeling, is our guide based on our life experiences and instinct. It can be very helpful when we listen to it and trust it. The problem is we often let our fear of the unknown and insatiable desire for certainty silence our intuition. It's always there, but we often can't hear it or are afraid to trust it. That's when we find ourselves seeking input from many others when we are unwilling or unable to move forward and make a decision on our own. We are so afraid of making the wrong choice that we become paralyzed and want others to tell us what we should do, and assure us that we aren't making a terrible mistake. It is only when we let go of our need for certainty that we will be able to listen to and trust our intuition to be our guide.

Our need for certainty can also stifle our creativity. Everyone is creative. The difference is that some people use their creativity while others don't. Brown states that "unused creativity doesn't just disappear. It lives within us until it's expressed, neglected to death, or suffocated by resentment and fear." When we are focused only on achieving perfection, we are constantly trying to keep up with those around us and comparing ourselves to them. That is exhausting to maintain and it certainly doesn't nurture our creative soul. We all place our own special and unique stamp on the world through our creativity. It's what makes us one of a kind. Our creativity allows us to be free of our perfectionist tendency to compare everything about us and our lives to others and just be our own unique selves.

How can we begin to let go of our need for certainty? These tips will help get you started:

- Recognize that there are no guarantees in life. You can never be certain of exactly how something will turn out. You can do what you can to prepare and hope for the best, but there will always be things beyond your control in play. The one constant in life is change, so, in essence, life itself is one big uncertainty.

- Remember that all you need is already within you. Too often we wait for something outside of us to come along and make us happy. We have the power to make it for ourselves. We don't need to wait for something good to come along. We can roll up our sleeves and create the life we want on our own.

- Don't hang on to the past so tightly that you miss out on the wonderful opportunities the future has to offer. As much as we feel connected and attached to our past, it is important to always keep an open mind about the possibility of even better things happening in the future.

- Focus on the things that matter most to you in life. What do you consider to be the biggest gifts in your life? What do you hold so dear that everything else pales in comparison? Most likely your answers included your family, friends, and good health. Without these, nothing else would matter much. They are the touchstones in your life on which you can depend. They can be a source of strength for you when you need it.

- Accept and appreciate that you, and your life, are perfectly imperfect. Don't keep holding out hope that there will be one day when you have your heart's every desire and everything will be perfect. Perfection is an illusion, so if you are waiting until you catch it to be happy, you will be sorely disappointed. Look for the little joys and happiness that can be found all around you.

Let Go of Productivity as a Sign of Self-Worth and as a Status Symbol

If you ever feel like there are more than enough hours in the day for you to accomplish everything that you'd like to, then you're probably not human! In today's fast-paced world, we are constantly trying to push ourselves to get more and more done in less time. Our to-do lists seem to be never-ending—we cross one thing off and three more are ready to take its place. We are constantly on the go and feel a greater sense of self-worth the more productive we are. Perfectionists feel this more strongly than perhaps anyone else. In striving for perfection, they often set the bar for their sense of self-worth as directly tied to how much they are able to accomplish, instead of recognizing that their feeling of self-worth can't come from anywhere other than inside themselves and it is earned simply by existing in the world. This makes the idea of them taking time off to just relax a very stressful thought.

They consider it to be a luxury they simply can't afford. But it turns out that play is something everyone should add to their to-do list. We typically think of play as being something that is good for children, but playing just for its own sake is very beneficial for adults as well. Play gives us the chance to take a break from all of the pressure we feel to be perfect and just take some time to relax and have fun.

We have a notion etched in our minds that being tired is a sort of status symbol because it is a sign that we have been working hard. We have the idea that success comes only from hard work ingrained in us from the time we are young. Great value is placed on being productive in the way that our society defines it. We often see rest, play, and even sleep as a waste of time and something that we can catch up on later. That is simply not the case. Being able to get an adequate amount of rest is essential, and being over-worked, over-stressed, and exhausted are impediments to our productivity and can often be hazardous to our health and well-being. Maybe the best path toward being productive isn't simply working harder—maybe it should be in setting priorities, consciously directing our work and efforts toward areas of our life that we value and that contribute to the way we want to live.

I have a quote framed in my office that says, "Success is knowing when to stop and play." This sits right above my desk and serves as a good reminder to me when I am tempted to just keep pushing through when I know my mind and body are letting me know that I need to take a break. It is through play that we can achieve our best work. Giving our bodies and brains a chance to relax and recharge allows us to come back to our work feeling refreshed and energized with a more positive perspective. It encourages us to keep our lives balanced and opens us up to more creative and innovative thoughts in the workplace. Play increases our feeling of satisfaction with our jobs and helps prevent burnout. It can help improve our social skills and relationships. Play requires a conscious choice on our part. We need to be willing to let go of our preconceived notions that exhaustion is a status symbol and that our productivity is a demonstration of our self-worth. We should embrace play for no other purpose than the sheer enjoyment it brings to our lives. We might just be surprised at the powerful difference it can make in healing our souls.

Let Go of Supposed-Tos and Self-Doubt

Perfectionists have an image in their minds of the way they feel they and their lives are supposed to be. When they are unable to live up to their impossibly high standards, they view themselves as a failure and begin to doubt themselves and their abilities. They don't view mistakes as opportunities to learn and grow, but rather see them as evidence that they just don't measure up to others.

To the outside observer, perfectionists may appear to be self-confident, but this is largely due to their efforts to maintain a perfect façade and not allow others to see their imperfections. Their self-confidence is fleeting since it is tied to gaining the acceptance and approval of others. As long as they are able to do this, their sense of self-worth remains intact, but as soon as they make mistakes that they think others can see, their self-confidence decreases. They feel as though they must constantly prove their worth and value to others. Perfectionists feel guilty when they think they have let others down, and that is when their self-doubt begins to take over.

This guilt and desire to please others even at the expense of losing our own true sense of self begins at an early age. I saw it regularly in my young students. On the occasions that I would let them grade their own papers and change any answers that they got wrong, my students struggled. Despite there being no negative consequence to getting an answer wrong, or even anyone else seeing it, the children would still try to hide their mistakes by feverishly erasing the incorrect answer and attempting to replace it with the correct one in such a way that no one could tell. They always wanted to be able to write that they hadn't missed any questions at the top of their paper. Even at a young age, they felt bad about making mistakes and wanted to hide them from others rather than simply learning from them.

This was also evident when they would conduct science experiments. The students always had to make a hypothesis before they began, which was their guess as to how they thought the experiment would turn out. I would explain to them that scientists view their experiments as trial and errors, and they don't mind being wrong or making mistakes because they see mistakes as stepping stones that teach them lessons and move them one step closer to the truth they seek. It never failed that every time my students made a hypothesis that was incorrect, they always tried to go back and change it to make it fit their experiment's results. They knew that they were not graded based on whether their hypothesis was right or wrong, and that I was fine if their original thinking was incorrect, but they were simply unable to just accept learning from a mistake. They had a very hard time letting it go.

If it's so difficult for our kids to overcome feelings of guilt and shame about making mistakes when they are young, imagine how hard it is for adults to shake their self-doubt after they have lived with it for many years. They become so afraid of making mistakes that they avoid trying new things. They miss out on many of the joys and opportunities that life has to offer and are held back from reaching their full potential.

How can we go about combatting our feelings of self-doubt? First, we need to understand how our brains work. There is a popular program in teaching children today about being "bucket fillers," which can help us understand. It says that when our buckets are full, we feel great, and that since we want everyone to feel good about themselves, we should try to fill their buckets too. We fill the buckets of others any time we show them compassion, love, and kindness. As we fill the buckets of other people through our good deeds and kind words and actions, we also fill up our own buckets as a result.

Think of your brain as having buckets in it as well. As you have positive life experiences and feelings, your buckets fill up. Perfectionists take longer to fill up their buckets because they only view perfection as being a desirable experience, so that filter through which they view the world keeps many experiences that others would enjoy, value, and consider successes from entering their buckets. These empty buckets keep perfectionists from having more positive feelings and allow self-doubt to enter their minds as they are unhappy that they aren't achieving the results they desire.

How can we increase what flows into our buckets so they can fill up faster and increase our feelings of self-confidence and joy?

- Enjoy the simple things, for one day you'll look back and realize they were the big things. Celebrate the small successes you experience. Something major doesn't always have to happen. Maybe you take time out to enjoy reading with your child, walk your dog, or go out to dinner with your significant other. If it brought you joy, it's a win and should go straight in your bucket.

- Think about an experience you recently had. You may not have immediately considered it a success because things didn't go exactly as you had planned or mistakes were made. Look at it through the lens that you view the people you care about the most with. If that same experience had happened to a dear friend or family member, would you have viewed it as positive? If so, lighten up on yourself and view your own experiences through the same lens as you do those you love. It is okay to set the same standard for success for yourself as you do everyone else (as long as it's realistic).

- Keep a gratitude journal and write down five things that you are thankful for each day. You will find that over time you become more aware of the little things that bring you joy in your life that you may not have been conscious of before.

- Step out of your comfort zone to try new things. Go to a new restaurant, go on vacation somewhere you have never been before, take a class on a hobby or topic that intrigues you, volunteer in your community, meet new people, or go to a party. While it may seem daunting at first, you may find out that you have hidden talents you were never aware of or enjoy things more than you ever thought you might.

Cultivate Laughter

Few things in life are as cathartic and healing as a good old-fashioned belly laugh shared with a friend. Sometimes laughter really is the best medicine. You can be holding on to all sorts of pent-up stress and then start laughing at even the slightest little thing. Chances are you won't be able to stop. Your shoulders will shake and tears may even start to roll from your eyes. And even if you can't fully understand what was so funny in the first place, I guarantee that you'll feel much better afterward. No matter the many differences in people and cultures around the world, we all laugh in the same language. It is part of our common human experience and it is truly healing for the soul.

Music and dance are two more things that transcend time and place and can unite us all by the feelings they evoke. I can hear a song and instantly be transported back to a memory—good or bad—that I remember vividly and it stirs up so many emotions. I would bet that you are probably the same way. Music is truly powerful.

Few things are so intimidating, or so freeing, as being able to let loose and burst out in song. Singing can bring us a feeling of great joy or bring us a sense of peace when it allows us to release sadness and pain. While I have been a part of more than a few choirs in my life, I will admit that I still find singing a solo, whether it be in church or with the karaoke machine, a nerve-wracking experience. There is something that makes sharing our voice with others an experience that can leave us feeling very vulnerable and exposed. That is why I prefer to save my solos for my family, or even better, myself in the shower or in my car.

When it comes to dance, I love dancing with my wife and children, as they are my safe place to land. I know that, while I hear a song and right away start swaying with the music or tapping my foot, my dancing skills are not stellar. I am willing to make a fool of myself around my family because I know that they will be laughing with me—not at me—when my lack of natural dance ability is on full display for all to see.

When laughter, song, and dance are such universal sources of joy and allow us to experience and express every human emotion, isn't it sad that we only participate in these activities when we feel the most at ease and aren't worried about how others will perceive, or even judge us? We might be well served to let go of our desire to appear perfect on the outside and follow some advice we learned in an earlier chapter: remember that no one cares that much about you. As much as it might feel as though everyone is staring at and judging us, the reality is that most of them aren't. They have their own problems and concerns, just like us, that they are more interested in. Even if they do recognize mistakes we are making, they will quickly be forgotten. It is easier said than done, but if we can learn to let go of our fears of letting our imperfections show and just enjoy the moment, we might uncover more happiness than we ever thought possible, and make some pretty amazing memories at the same time.

Key Takeaways:

- Being authentic means letting go of the image of what we think we should be, and being willing to share our true selves with others—imperfections and all. We become more authentic when we take the time to really get to know ourselves and others, when we truly listen to the people around us and give them the attention they deserve as we are present in the moment, and when we stop wasting our time trying to be perfect.

- Compassion isn't only something we should show to others—we should be willing to show it to ourselves as well. After all, one thing that we all have in common is that none of us are perfect.

- Everyone has perfectionist tendencies within themselves to varying degrees. The first step in overcoming them is becoming more self-aware.

- Our fear of the unknown can cause us to become stagnant and unwilling to try new things as it stifles our intuition and creativity. This prevents us from learning and growing to reach our full potential and causes us to miss out on many of the amazing opportunities that life has to offer.

- When we spend less time being worried about what others think of us and more time living in the moment, we discover who we really are and experience more joy than we ever thought possible.

Chapter 6: How Much of a Perfectionist Are You?

As we have discussed, we all have perfectionist tendencies within us to varying degrees. The first step to overcoming those tendencies and living our best life is to face them head on as we become more self-aware. Take a moment to take the test below to discover a little more about yourself and see where you fall on the perfectionist continuum. For each question below, select the choice that best describes or applies to you.

		Strongly disagree	Disagree	Somewhat disagree /agree	Agree	Strongly agree
		1	2	3	4	5
1.	I'm only happy if what I do receives praise from others.	○	○	○	○	○
2.	I prefer to do things myself because I know they will be done right.	○	○	○	○	○

3. When I reflect on my life so far, I see more failures than successes.	○	○	○	○	○
4. Receiving negative feedback makes me feel like I am a failure.	○	○	○	○	○
5. I am only satisfied when everything goes perfectly according to my plan.	○	○	○	○	○

6. I think it's important to be perfect so I won't be rejected by others.	○	○	○	○	○
7. The thought of being average at something makes me feel awful.	○	○	○	○	○
8. If I make a mistake at work, my boss will be disappointed in me	○	○	○	○	○

and think I'm incompetent.					
9. I feel pressure to constantly surpass my boss's expectations at work and outperform my colleagues.	○	○	○	○	○

10.	No matter how hard I try to please others, I feel like what I do isn't good enough.	○	○	○	○	○
11.	I consider performing satisfactorily at work to be a failure on my part.	○	○	○	○	○
12.	If my children aren't successful in school and extra-	○	○	○	○	○

	curricular activities, I am not a good parent.				
13.	I should excel at everything I do.	○	○ ○	○	○
14.	I am proud of the things I have accomplished in my life.	○	○ ○	○	○
15.	The thought of making a mistake really bothers me.	○	○ ○	○	○

16.	I am greatly concerned with how I am perceived by others.	○	○ ○	○	○
17.	It takes me a long time to let go of criticism that I receive from others.	○	○ ○	○	○
18.	I have trouble saying no to others because I don't want to let them down.	○	○ ○	○	○

19.	I would have to be in perfect physical shape to be considered attractive.	○	○ ○	○	○
20.	If a group project I'm involved in is unsuccessful, it's usually due to a lack of effort from the other members of the group.	○	○ ○		○

Now it is time to analyze your results. Add up the number of total points you scored to see where you fall on the perfectionist continuum.

80-100: Absolute Perfectionist

Your perfectionism is having a major, and often negative, impact on your life. You feel as though you are not good enough and can't measure up to others. Your critical inner voice is working overtime pointing out all of your mistakes and flaws. You are very hard on yourself. Your sense of self-worth and self-confidence are suffering and you have a hard time accepting praise for your work because you always think you should have done better. You doubt yourself and are hesitant to try new things because you are afraid of making a mistake. You can definitely benefit from showing yourself some of the same compassion you show to those you love and from reaching out to your support system. Practice the tips and strategies in this book and remember that you are worthy of love and respect just by existing in the world. The 7.5 billion people on the planet aren't perfect and you don't have to be either!

60-79: Moderate Perfectionist

Your perfectionism has an influence on the way you see yourself and the world and on your relationships with others. It is usually not a serious problem for you, but it does cause you some unnecessary stress and anxiety at times. You are not an extreme perfectionist, but there are times when your high standards and expectations can be unrealistic. Remember to continue to get to know yourself, and work toward being less concerned with the way others think of you and more concerned with taking time to stop and play and with embracing your imperfections.

40-59: Balanced Perfectionist

You are usually successful at keeping your perfectionist tendencies in check. There may be times when your critical inner voice tries to convince you that you are not good enough, but you are able to tune it out and ignore it. Continue to be self-aware and you will be able to maintain your healthy level of perfectionism.

20-39: Indifferent Perfectionist

Your perfectionist tendencies may come into play on occasion in your life, but they are not a concern for you. Your rejection of society's expectations and standards of perfection can be a healthy choice as long as you set more, high yet reasonable, standards for yourself to act as motivation for you in your life. Remember that it is always beneficial to challenge yourself to reach beyond your comfort zone as you strive to learn and grow. Be open to trying new things and committed to building strong healthy relationships.

Chapter 7: The 30-Day Perfectionism Cure

Here we are, equipped with knowledge and self-knowledge about perfectionist tendencies. We understand its roots, manifestations, and consequences on our lives. We gained awareness. That's an essential first step. But just because we know all that we know after reading this book, it won't vanish our perfectionism. We need to put in the work. It is life-long work, really, but once the anti-perfectionism practices turn into habits, they won't require much effort from our side. Perfectionism robs us of much more energy, time, and joy than the habits meant to diminish it. So, don't worry. All that we learn next is a net positive on the effort scale.

This chapter will guide you through practices aimed to develop such habits. It might be uncomfortable or unnatural at first. Still, if you stick to the exercises in the next 30 days, you'll see how much easier they become over time. They don't require much of your time. That's the beauty of them.

Without further ado, let's get started!

"You were born to be real, not to be perfect. You are here to be you, not to live someone else's life."

-

Ralph Martson

Days 1–3: Noting, Naming, and Releasing

Meditation practice includes a simple method called "noting" or "labeling." When you sit down to meditate, your thoughts will soon invade your mind. At that moment, you have two choices regarding how to go on with your practice. You will either feel upset and judgment about how imperfectly you meditate, or you can choose to gently acknowledge what is happening in the present. Note "thinking" in your mind, give it space, and then gently let the thoughts go. The second option is what we call "noting." It's a gentle shift of focus onto what's happening, accepting it, and releasing it.

I would like you to do the same thing whenever you catch yourself having an urge to do something perfectly. For example, you just sat down comfortably on your couch to read after cleaning the entire kitchen. When you lean to grab your book, you notice that you forgot to put your coffee mug into the dishwasher. The kitchen, thus, is not in perfect order. You have this urge to get up and put the coffee mug away. You tell yourself the story that you can't relax otherwise. Clutter will bug you. This was a personal example, but I'm sure that you frequently experience some version of this "problem."

Let's approach the event differently. Using the technique of noting, instead of jumping up and executing the perfectionist mind's order, just note to yourself, "perfection-seeking." You can even talk to your perfectionism (out loud if you're comfortable with it). "I see you, perfectionism. I see what you're trying to do here. I accept what you're wishing to do.

Thank you for your observation, but I don't need to put the mug away at this moment. I can relocate it the next time I'm getting up. And if I forget it, I will wash this mug by hand or in the next dishwashing round."

Talk to your perfectionist mind. Don't belittle it, don't judge it. Simply state what the right mind wants. You will be surprised about how much ease and peace of mind this simple technique can bring to you. Notice the perfectionist urge, name it, and state your true wishes without self-judgment.

You can do this practice with small things like a misplaced mug. Gradually move toward things with a greater consequence, such as a work project or having The Talk with your teenage child. In fact, you should start small and build up the comfort of noting, naming, and releasing.

I chose to add this practice to Days 1–3 because this is the foundational stone to all the other exercises. This is an exercise I encourage you to do every day from now on. Make a post-it saying "Noting, Naming, and Releasing," and stick it onto a visible place. It takes less than a minute, but without being able to catch yourself before engaging in a perfectionist act, you will have difficulty overcoming it.

Days 4–6: Perfectionism Diary

Let's take the "Noting, Naming, and Releasing" technique a step further. Assign a little notebook, or a memo in your phone, to record the perfectionism urges you've noticed. If you are using paper, create the following template. If you are using your phone, write out each element on separate lines. I filled out one line with the mug example from yesterday.

Date and Time	Event	Perfectionism Urge (1-10)	Feelings, Thoughts, Actions

	1.01.	I forgot to place the coffee mug into the dish-washer.	3-4	I felt restless, I thought the room was messy, I wanted to jump up to fix the "problem" but I kept my composure and just noted my experience instead.

Keep this template at hand and try to do your best (but not perfect) effort to journal and record your perfectionist urges for the next 30 days. If you're consistent with this work, eventually, some patterns of habits will emerge. Take a good look at your patterns.

• What kind of activity/task/event triggers your perfectionist instinct most often?
• How do you usually react to it?
• What time of the day is your "perfectionist" zone?
• How intensely do you feel the urge? How hard is it to control it?

For example, you will see that you could successfully overcome an urge of 3-4, like the coffee mug. But how well did you do with a desire of 7-8? If you succeeded in warding off this intense impulse, it might have come at a tremendous emotional cost. Notice all these details about your behavior. Track them week by week. You will see that, gradually, the more you repeat and succeed in overcoming a smaller urge, the more significant impulses will be overcome as well.

The benefit of this written exercise over the mental-noting technique is its trackability and visual impact. It's one thing to notice and mentally release a perfectionist urge and another to actually see its frequency, impact, and importance, and to measure your progress in doing better.

Days 7–9: Urge—Thought—Emotion Triangle

You want to do something perfectly because of an underlying emotion triggering it. This emotion is most commonly a fear of something: fear of rejection, fear of not being enough, fear of abandonment, fear of getting ridiculed, and so on.

But there is a bridge between the urge and the emotion, and this bridge is the story you tell yourself—your thoughts, in other words.

Today's task is to identify the stories you tell yourself about why you need to do each perfectionist action. You can use your most recent examples from the chart from Days 4–6 to make this exercise easier. Or you can think about perfectionist urges from your past.

Here is the flow of this practice. Recreate the following chart in your notebook or phone. First, fill in the Urge section, then identify and fill in the Emotion section. Finally, think about what story, belief, or conviction you have that connects your urges with your emotions.

Urge	Thought(s)	Emotion(s)
Put the cup in the dishwasher.	My belief is that my outer world reflects my inner world. Therefore, if my house is messy, people will judge me	Feeling of overwhelm, fear of judgment (for being messy).

	because of that—not only for the visible mess but they will also think that I'm lazy, incompetent, and unreliable.	

This is a powerful practice where you can learn a lot about the inner workings of your mind.

Days 10–12: Guiding Beliefs, Principles, and Convictions

Based on your work in the first nine days and your perfectionist urges in general, try to excavate some core beliefs you hold about yourself, the world, and other people. Try to find at least five.

Write them down.

For example:

> 1. I believe one's house reflects their inner qualities as a person.
> 2. I believe I am judged by others if the house is not neat.

3. I believe I am worth as much as the control I exert over my life.

4. I believe I must always keep my standards up. Otherwise, people will think that I'm not good enough.

5. I value order and discipline.

These are my personal discoveries around the cup affair. Do the same thing for your perfectionist urges. Suppose you identified some of a different nature, for example. In that case, one urge is about doing flawless work. The other is about showing up as the perfect partner. Try to make a list of five beliefs for both. They probably stem from different roots.

Days 13–15: Your Core Belief

Take a look at your list(s) from Days 10–12. You wrote five different, but related, beliefs that are connected to one of your perfectionist urges. Reread them. Usually, one of these beliefs is a core belief, and the others are little branches growing out from that core belief.

Imagine this like a tree. The core belief is the tree trunk, the related thoughts are the branches. Suppose we want to shift our belief (ultimately, that's what we need to do). In that case, we need to identify the one which would yield the greatest return on our time and effort investment.

How do we identify which is the core belief? Sometimes it is simple. If you have a statement such as "I am worthless," that is pretty deep and naked. But sometimes, it is not so obvious to fish out the core belief behind perfectionist urges. Maybe you didn't even mention the core belief in your five examples in the previous exercise. Perhaps all of them were branches.

Worry not, today the core belief will not escape. To identify it, we need to ask some additional questions. I will lead you through this exercise using my own example from yesterday.

> 1. I believe one's house reflects their inner qualities as a person.
> 2. I believe I am judged by others if the house is not neat.
> 3. I believe I am worth as much as the control I exert over my life.

4. I believe I must always keep my standards up. Otherwise, people will think that I'm not good enough.
5. I value order and discipline.

A good way to scrutinize your examples is to ask the question, "What does this mean?" For instance, I said, "I believe one's house reflects their inner qualities as people." What does that mean? That means that if I don't keep military order in my house, it is a sign that something's wrong with me. If I was well, I would keep the house in perfect order. Conversely, if I can't manage to keep the expected order despite my best efforts, I'm deficient somehow. I can't measure up; I am not good enough …

"I believe I am judged by others if the house is not neat." What does that mean? It means that people will see my imperfections if I allow space for that; they will see it, and then they will conclude, "Ah, this Steven guy is not worth it. He's not good enough to be my friend, colleague, spouse …"

"I believe I am worth as much as the control I exert over my life." What does that mean? It means that if I can't control my life, the space around me, I will come off as some inadequate person who is incapable of holding it together. People would think they can't count and rely on me, that I am not good enough to be an example or a stronghold for them.

I could go on, but I already see a common theme emerging—the one of not being good enough. This belief is the reason behind all my micromanaging, perfectionist tendencies around the house.

What are yours?

Days 16–18: Find the Origin Story of Your Core Beliefs

Now that you've identified some of your core beliefs that trigger your perfectionist tendencies, try to remember where you picked these beliefs up.

Was it at home? At school? Were your parents instilling the belief in you? Did you pick it up secondhand by, for example, observing how your parents related to each other?

Write about the origins of your core beliefs as extensively as possible.

For example, I bring my belief of not being enough—and its manifestation—from my grandmother. She was always obsessed with being clean; otherwise, the village people would badmouth her. And she was badmouthing friends whose houses she visited. She failed to see that her own judgment of others brought the fear of being judged onto her. As a child, I internalized that people who have a messy house are not good enough—or bad enough to be gossiped about by a sharp-tongued old woman. Don't get me wrong, my grandmother was a wonderful, caring woman who grew up in this mentality herself. She just passed on her baggage unknowingly.

After you identify your core belief's origin story, see if it is following your true values. Is that a core belief you want to keep?

Some core beliefs we hold are good and productive. For example, striving to be kind.

You may have learned that from your mom and you may want to hold on to that. But what about the core belief, "I am deficient or not good enough"? Do you genuinely believe that's the case? Do you want to keep believing that?

If not, it's time to question them and affirm that you want to change.

Days 19–21: Change Your Core Beliefs

In the last three days, you dug out the origin story of your core beliefs and chose the ones you'd like to change. In the following three days, you're going to do just that.

Write down the core belief you'd like to rewire.

For example, I feel like I am not good enough.

Now, write down what you would like to believe in a short, positive, affirmative sentence.

For example, I am good enough. Or I feel good about myself. Or I appreciate myself.

Make sure to be honest and realistic. Saying something like, "I am the best person alive," or "I will never feel like I don't measure up again," are not reasonable or realistic goals.

Do you have the positive affirmation? Time to use your inbuilt confirmation bias for something productive. Your task for the next three days will be to find instances that prove your positive affirmation. For example, my wife complimented me on my lasagna the other day. She said she is lucky to have a husband who cooks so well. This is definitely proof of being good enough.

Try to collect at least ten pieces of proof affirming your new core belief.

1.
2.

3.

4.

5.

6.

7.

8.

9.

10.

Days 22–24: Remove the Cues Triggering Your Perfectionist Habits

By this point, you have a list of the new core beliefs you want for yourself. You also have at least ten things that prove that your new core belief actually describes you perfectly (pun intended). This is a great start.

However, to consolidate your new core belief and unlearn the perfectionist habits related to your old core belief takes more work than writing a list of ten pieces of proof.

You may notice that even if you question your old story—for example, "I'm not good enough," and you state, "I know, in fact, that I am enough"—you still engage in the perfectionist habit. For example, I know that my wife and kids love and appreciate me dearly. They would love me even if I starred in an episode of *Hoarders*. Yet, I still find myself incessantly cleaning and sometimes organizing, knowing all that I know.

Chances are, you will sometimes re-engage in your perfectionist habits, even if you've successfully avoided them for a long time. And hey, that is awesome! We are not seeking the perfect obliteration of perfectionism here, right? But we can do our best to minimize and mitigate its impact.

James Clear, the author of the book *Atomic Habits*, advises us to make a habit we want to leave behind unattractive and difficult to do. Conversely, we should make a habit we want to enforce attractive and easy. How do you make your perfectionist habits unattractive and difficult to do?

> 1. Make a list of all the things that you are missing out on, renouncing, losing, and trading to make room for the perfectionist habit.

In my case, I surrender my comfort so easily. When I get in deep clean mode, I sometimes get exhausted by 10 am and have much less energy for the meaningful things I would do afterward.

2. Make a list of the emotions your perfectionist habit triggers in you.

3. What can you do to make your habit hard to perform?

For example, if you are a clean freak like me, you can collect all your cleaning gadgets, put them in a box, bring them up to your attic, garage, or storage room, and hide them. Make access difficult. In our household, we have a big box for my cleaning stuff in the garage with a lock. My wife has the key to that lock, and she opens the magic box every Sunday at 4 pm. 4–6 pm is my designated cleaning time for the week. It's silly, but it works! Find a way to create a similar barricade for yourself.

Follow your perfectionist habits for the next three days. Notice what the primary cues that make that habit easy are. Design a plan to make the habit unattractive and hard to perform.

Days 25–27: Add Cues That Facilitate Your New Habits

If you remove something from your life, something else will fill that void. Ideally, something positive, productive, and utterly imperfect should take the place of the perfectionist habit.

Let's take the next three days to design these new habits. The two things you should focus on are making the habit attractive and easy to perform.

1. What benefits would this new, imperfectionist habit bring into your life?

You can turn this new habit into a healthy version of the old, perfectionist habit. For example, suppose your old perfectionist habit was work-related. In that case, you can't ditch it and change it into something totally unrelated to your work. Your tasks should be executed and finished. How could you turn the bad habit around and make it into a good habit? For example, if you spent a lot of time revising your projects, emails, or other obligations, make a commitment to revisit it only once. Rereading something before sending it is actually a smart thing to do. You can even get a free extension like Grammarly on your desktop so that the app could automatically show you typos and weird wording problems. This would help you a lot with your tendency to deep-scan your text.

You could look at your decreased revision time as a benefit. Reward yourself somehow for it.

Take a more extended lunch break. Go home earlier, if you're allowed. Make sure to feel a positive difference in your life, thanks to the habit change.

2. How would you like to feel after performing this habit?

Calmer? More satisfied? Like you did the right thing? Proud? Meditate a bit on the outcome, the reward you want to get, and plan your habit accordingly.

3. Make it easy.

The example in point 1 is a good one for this. Do you want to spend less time obsessing over spelling? Get a good spell checker. Do you want to take your vitamins daily? Leave them on the main kitchen counter where you make your morning coffee.

Spend these three days with the design and formation of the new habits. Make them easy and attractive, and repeat them as often as you can.

Days 28–30: Notice the Rewards of a Less Perfect Life

Gratitude and appreciation are things that lift our spirit and make us feel better about ourselves, people, and life in general. I would like to end this program by inviting you to think about three things you feel grateful for regarding your hard work to overcome perfectionism.

What am I grateful for in my current life?
1.
2.
3.

What rewards do I experience in life thanks to my new, imperfectionist habits?

1.
2.
3.

I want to thank myself for:

1.
2.
3.

Fill in these lines three days in a row. Think about how your life is now compared to when you started this program. Set new goals, milestones, and aspirations for the future. Track your habits and urges. Get to know yourself better.

Congratulations on making it here! Good luck in the future!

Closing

Perfectionist tendencies exist within all of us to varying degrees. When we forget to show ourselves the same understanding and compassion that we offer our loved ones and are unnecessarily hard on ourselves, perfectionism becomes maladaptive and harmful. We become afraid to step outside of our comfort zone and try new things. This can make us miss out on the many attractive opportunities and joy life has to offer.

In this book, we worked hard to get to know ourselves and understand when we are tempted to let our desire to please others win. We became more self-aware and learned adaptive responses to keep these tendencies balanced and in check. As we progress, we'll gain confidence that our perfectionism can be maintained at a healthy level. This is beneficial in our lives, serving as appropriate motivation to achieve success and reach realistically high standards.

It certainly won't be easy, and it will take a life-long commitment on our part to try to overcome our perfectionist tendencies every day. Still, it is possible to have a healthy relationship with perfection and come through the other side, stronger. Good luck to you!

Steven

Reference

Benson, Etienne. The many faces of perfectionism. American Psychological Association. 2003. http://www.apa.org/monitor/nov03/manyfaces.aspx

Brown, Brene. The Gifts of Imperfection. Hazelden Publishing. 2010.

Laack, Davis, Paula. 5 Styles of Perfectionism. Paula Davis Laack. 2018. https://www.pauladavislaack.com/5-styles-of-perfectionism/

Lombardo, Elizabeth, PhD. 9 Signs That You Might Be a Perfectionist. Psychology Today. 2016. https://www.psychologytoday.com/us/blog/better-perfect/201611/9-signs-you-might-be-perfectionist

Packard, E. Perfectionists more vulnerable to depression, study finds. American Psychological Association. 2006. http://www.apa.org/monitor/may06/perfectionists.aspx

Rice, K. G., Choi, C.-C., Zhang, Y., Morero, Y. I., & Anderson, D. (2012). Self-Critical Perfectionism, Acculturative Stress, and Depression Among International Students. *The Counseling Psychologist*, *40*(4), 575–600. https://doi.org/10.1177/0011000011427061

Endnotes

---

[i] Packard, E. Perfectionists more vulnerable to depression, study finds. American Psychological Association. 2006. http://www.apa.org/monitor/may06/perfectionists.aspx

[ii] Rice, K. G., Choi, C.-C., Zhang, Y., Morero, Y. I., & Anderson, D. (2012). Self-Critical Perfectionism, Acculturative Stress, and Depression Among International Students. *The Counseling Psychologist, 40*(4), 575–600. https://doi.org/10.1177/0011000011427061

[iii] Brown, Brene. The Gifts of Imperfection. Hazelden Publishing. 2010.

[iv] Brown, Brene. The Gifts of Imperfection. Hazelden Publishing. 2010.

www.ingramcontent.com/pod-product-compliance
Lightning Source LLC
Chambersburg PA
CBHW052042280426
43661CB00085B/55